Stumpwork
The Art of Raised Embroidery

STUMPWORK

The Art of Raised Embroidery

Muriel Baker

Charles Scribner's Sons
New York

Library of Congress Cataloging in Publication Data
Baker, Muriel L.
    Stumpwork.

    Includes Index.
    1. Stump work.   I. Title.
TT778.S75B34   746.4'4   77-13204
ISBN 0-684-15360-2

The selection from *Historical Needlework* by Margaret Swain
is used with the permission of Charles Scribner's Sons
and Barrie & Jenkins, copyright © 1970 Margaret H. Swain.

1 3 5 7 9 11 13 15 17 19 MD/C 20 18 16 14 12 10 8 6 4 2

Printed in the United States of America

ACKNOWLEDGMENTS

There are so many people who contribute to any endeavor of this sort. I would like to give special thanks to my pupils, whose great interest in and enthusiasm for stumpwork inspired me to write this book. My sister, Marion Lewis, helped me in so many ways that I could not possibly list them all! Four photographers supplied the beautiful color plates: Harold Pratt, Marion Lewis, Douglas Armsden, and Sally Chapman. I am envious of their expertise and I thank them for their efforts. Barbara Eyre's exceptional talents are evident in the line drawings and some of the designs. Heather Clark worked many long hours on the stitch charts, as did Jeanne Simpson on typing the manuscript. A special bow to Anne Dyer, one of England's foremost needlewomen, who did much work for me in England. Jean Mailey and Barbara Teague of the Metropolitan Museum of Art were most patient and most helpful. And, of course, a special thank you to all those who allowed me to share their beautiful work with you. My manuscript would never have become a book without Elinor Parker, my editor, and I hereby extend to her my gratitude.

MURIEL L. BAKER

ontents

List of Color Plates

This is a mirror surround from Strangers' Hall in Norwich, England. The figures represent the King and Queen and are seen beneath canopies whose curtains draw! Stumpwork figures are often seen beneath canopies or tents and more often than not the little curtains draw. In the seventeenth century, tents were always taken along on journeys, and they were raised against the elements for noble personages whenever the cavalcade rested. Photo by Hallam Ashley.

Life in Seventeenth-Century England

To UNDERSTAND STUMPWORK, one should know something of the history and manners of Stuart England in the 1600s. This period falls naturally into three parts: the reign of Charles I and his Queen, Henrietta Maria; the Commonwealth under the guidance of Oliver Cromwell; and finally the days of Charles II and his Queen, Catherine of Braganza.

For the most part, despite the civil war and the Commonwealth (1642–1660), these were happy times in England. Most of the people were well fed, well housed, and contented with their lot. Even the poor were taken care of. There was a Poor Law which levied a tax to be used for the care of the poor, and the Overseers of the Poor in every city and parish were called upon to buy materials to provide work for the unemployed.

It was a great period for the so-called gentry, the country squires. They were active in all facets of society and their ranks were constantly changing. Class distinctions were accepted as a matter of course without jealousy in any sector. The classes were not rigid nor were they strictly hereditary. Persons moved from one class to another by the acquisition of wealth, property, or perhaps a change of occupation. The social order was based on equality of opportunity and great freedom. The so-called Peers of the Realm represented only a small section of the people; they enjoyed great personal prestige and many privileges. They were expected to maintain great households. Their lovely and commodious dwellings spread over the English countryside, most of them built by the preceding generation. These great estates were best described as little towns within themselves and were largely self-supporting.

The master of the household had little to do but enjoy a life of leisure; he was conditioned to enjoy life to the fullest. He spent his days shooting game, hunting fox and stag, netting birds, and enjoying swordplay, bull and bear baiting, and cockfighting. He and his entire household visited spas from time to time because it was the thing to do, and also for reasons of health; the royal court moved each year to Tunbridge Wells, for example.

The lady of the household spent leisurely days at fine and coarse needlework of various sorts, as well as embroidery. Within the household there were often poor relations, known as "lady helps," who did the fine cooking, the preserving, the preparing of medicines, the making of jams, jellies, syrups, and wines. These "lady helps" were also adept at the spinning wheel and the weaving loom.

The servants baked, brewed, churned, ground meal, took care of poultry and pigeons, slaughtered and cured the cattle and pigs. There were carpenters and there were paint shops, brew houses, dairies where horses turned the huge churns, dovecotes, and fishponds. These households were well provisioned, with chickens, rabbits, beef, lamb, pork, and deer in great quantity. Gentlemen ate white bread, the servants dark. Meat and bread were the chief foods with few vegetables, although "sallets" (salads) were becoming popular. Sugar was imported, and puddings were a very well-thought-of dish. Dinner was the main meal, eaten between eleven and twelve, followed by supper some four or five hours later. Enormous quantities of food were consumed at these meals.

The dress of both men and women "of quality" was rich, expensive, and very elaborate.

The members of the so-called yeoman class, which comprised four-fifths of the population, were for the most part farmers for the gentlemen. During the seventeenth century, however, an increasing proportion of the population became engaged in trade or took up some situation in industry. Small businesses were on the increase. Trade with

India was flourishing and the merchant class was increasing in importance all the time.

The war between the Cavaliers and the Roundheads, which resulted in the Cromwellian Revolution, was a political and religious conflict. The men who were responsible for it had no desire to change the social order or to redistribute the nation's wealth; it was essentially a war of ideas. The lords and the gentlemen (Cavaliers) were on the side of the King, as were the inhabitants of the market towns farthest away from the capital. These Cavaliers were generally easygoing folk who expected to enjoy life to its fullest. Those on the side of Cromwell and Parliament (Roundheads) were in general the yeomen and townsfolk as well as those from the rural areas. The Roundheads idealized business and enterprise and believed in hard work as opposed to the easygoing life of the Cavaliers.

The Restoration in 1660 restored the nobles to their hereditary place as the leaders of society and unfortunately started a class cleavage that had not existed before.

The court under Charles II, who was known as Merry King Charles, was flamboyant and gay beyond belief. Anything went, and although England itself was sound, there was a great lack of belief in virtue throughout the land, especially in the upper classes. Charles was a noted patron of the arts, especially the theater, which was centered in London and existed primarily for the entertainment of the court and the city fashionables.

Under King Charles II the deterioration of the great estates began to take place. Samuel Pepys wrote in his diary that "our gentry are grown ignorant in everything of good husbandry."

In 1665 London lost one-fifth of its population to the Great Plague. And in 1666 the Great Fire, which burned for five days, ravaged London, destroying the Tudor city. But through the combined efforts of the King and Parliament the city was rebuilt and regained its place in the social and economic scheme of things in England.

Overall, despite the war and the period of adjustment following it, the reign of the Stuarts in England was a period of tranquillity, social growth, and achievement.

The clothing of the time was truly worthy of note; at no time in history was it richer, more opulent. A gentleman's suit consisted of doublet, breeches, and mandilion or cloak. The doublet, which was worn over the shirt, was close-fitting, long-waisted, and often boned. More often than not it was lined, and sometimes quilted. It dipped to a sharp point in the front and was studded with pairs of eyelets for attaching the breeches. If the owner was wealthy, his doublet was fastened by rows of closely set buttons; if not, by pins. Many times the doublets were gaily decorated. Four- to six-inch-long vertical slashes, called panes, were located over the breast area, and brightly colored lining showed in the gaps. Often these garments were covered with elaborate embroidery and festooned with braid.

The sword belt was elaborately decorated and narrow, and it followed the contour of the waist. It must be remembered that everything was made to order, that nothing was for sale "off the racks." A gentleman might have several coats, among them a mandilion, a long, loose-fitting garment with a standing collar, which was put on over the head. He certainly would have a cloak, circular in cut, lined with

velvet, which would match his doublet and breeches. A cloak was considered essential for appearing in public.

Two kinds of neckwear were popular: the collar and the ruff. Sometimes the collar or band was small and turned down; sometimes it was standing. Usually collars were made of linen, but neither lace nor lawn was uncommon. The ruffs were also of two varieties: the standing, made up of layers of single ruffled bands tied together in front; and the falling, which drooped and was made up of gathered layers of linen or lawn.

Stockings reached above the knee and were knitted in silk if one was wealthy, and in various other threads if not. They were very gay,

5

Men's clothing was very elaborate in the 1600s. Here are some typical costumes of the times.

in green, scarlet, russet, yellow, silver, or blue, and were a much-prized article of apparel. They were very bulky and were held up by garters tied in a large bow below the knee.

Shoes had either round or square toes and raised heels, often colored red, and they were made of leather. When they were laced it was with ribbon, which was very often decorated with spangles. And of course every gentleman had a pair of exquisite boots with spurs for outdoor wear. These were made of the finest leather. Caps, embroidered or decorated in some fashion, were worn indoors and on all formal occasions. Great broad-brimmed hats with high crowns were worn cocked (turned up) outdoors.

Men wore their hair full; bushy-tight curls all over the head were most favored. Wigs became popular about 1650 and were considered a necessity at court.

The lady of the household wore a gown, enhanced by a farthingale and a stomacher, with a low-necked bodice, corset-like and heavily

boned. Sometimes in place of the bodice a doublet or jacket was worn. The doublet was very fashionable. It was more comfortable than the bodice because it was not boned. It was close-fitting, however, despite the fact that it flared sharply from the waist. It was fastened with buttons or ribbons, had close-fitting sleeves with cuffs of lace, lawn, or linen, and was more often than not heavily embroidered.

The shape of the gown's skirt depended on the farthingale. There were two popular kinds: the wheel farthingale and the roll. The wheel, as its name implies, was wheel-shaped and made of either wire or whalebone. The wearer's waist formed the hub of the wheel, which spread out about the hips. It tilted down in front and up behind. The roll farthingale, which made the wearer look very plump, was a

7

Some typical women's dresses of the 1600s.

padded roll, or sometimes several padded rolls sewed together. Sometimes it was the manner to wear gowns without farthingales. When this was the case, the skirt was "bunched up" to show the elegant petticoats underneath.

Women also wore cloaks as outer garments. These were frequently fur-lined with deep, turned-down collars that could serve as hoods. It was fashionable to be bareheaded outdoors during the seventeenth century. However, various types of headcloths were sometimes worn. The most popular with the ladies was the coronet, which was oblong-shaped with squared ends, made from linen, lace, or velvet. When made from linen the coronet was beautifully embroidered. Head rails, arched hoods, and head kerchiefs were also favored, the arched hood being used by the elderly or by those in mourning. A coif was a close-fitting hood much like a baby's bonnet. It was becoming to most and therefore very popular, and when it was embroidered it made a handsome addition to the wearer's costume. Cauls, elaborately decorated, were worn at the back of the head.

The hair styles of the times were of special interest to the embroideress, as she fashioned her small figures with so much skill and care. In the most elaborate style the hair was brushed up high from the forehead and temples over a pad or a built-up wire support. In another popular fashion the hair was curled, brushed up straight back from the forehead, and then fluffed out around the cheeks. Sometimes the curls were so arranged that they looked as if they were stuck down across the wearer's forehead. In yet another favored style the hair was brushed straight back over two side partings at the temples. Then unbelievable corkscrew curls fell to shoulder length. These painstakingly wrought coiffures were decorated with pearls or other precious jewels, feathers, or lace.

It was the fashion to wear much makeup, and black patches were a necessary adornment.

Ladies' shoes and stockings were similar to those worn by the gentlemen of the period and also featured red heels. The red heels are often seen in the embroideries.

Much jewelry was worn—necklaces, long gold chains, earrings, bracelets, and large showy rings, which were worn on the fourth finger and often tied to the wrist by a chain.

A few of the many intriguing hair styles of the period.

Then there was the curious use of face masks. These covered the entire face and were held in place by a round bead attached to the inner surface and kept between the teeth! Half-masks which covered only the upper half of the face were also popular. They were more conventionally secured by ties.

Certainly this colorful dress, both male and female, made interesting subjects for the embroideress. It is obvious that she spent many hours making many careful stitches, rendering perfect likenesses of the dress of the times. It is a feature of stumpwork.

A crucifix, originally used as an orphrey cross on the back of a chasuble, made in Germany in the fifteenth century. The figures are beautifully delineated in raised work, with very close attention to the faces and hands. In general, the figures on these ecclesiastical pieces from the Continent are superior to the English ones. Courtesy of the Art Institute of Chicago.

Stumpwork

IT WAS AGAINST THIS BACKGROUND that the embroideress picked up her needle. On her frame was stitched a piece of heavy white satin on which were stamped myriad figures, flowers, animals, and insects arranged in an intriguing design. Beside her lay another piece of fabric, stout linen, also tautly stretched, on which were stamped small figures and animals. On her work table colored silks and various metallic threads vied with the jewels, pieces of lace, brocade, mica, and other bits of finery for her attention. She was about to begin a piece of stumpwork. It has been said that stumpwork was the sampler work of young ladies. There seems no evidence that it was sampler work but rather much evidence that it was the leisure pastime of wealthy ladies.

Even the name *stumpwork* is suspect. John L. Nevison, writing in the *Catalogue of English Domestic Embroidery*, published by the Victoria and Albert Museum in 1938, has this to say in regard to the commonly used term. In 1688 an encyclopedic book of embroidery stitches and techniques was published: *The Academy of Armoury*, compiled by Randall Holme. Nevison states that in that book "there is no mention of 'stumpwork' which is to-day the generally accepted name for the raised and padded embroidery used for pictures, looking-glass frames and work boxes." The *Oxford Dictionary*, however, surprisingly quotes the first use of the word from the *Burlington Magazine* in 1904. And an earlier instance has since

In the lower left-hand corner of this painting is the type of frame that was used in the seventeenth century. Museum of Art, Rhode Island School of Design, Providence, R.I.

been found in F. and H. Marshall's *Old English Embroidery* (1894), while Lady Marian Alford in *Needlework as Art* (1886) speaks of "the style of work called embroidery on the stamp which was then the fashion." The contemporary name for this work was "raised work," a name that is commonly found in writings of the period.

If use of a name through the years gives it stature, then *stumpwork* is not a misnomer for this embroidery style, which originated on the continent of Europe, where it was used extensively for ecclesiastical purposes in Italy, Spain, Germany, and France. Many of these pieces were altar frontals. The raised or "embost work" was used to empha- size the design, provide clarity, and give dramatic quality. Work of this kind was common in the fifteenth century, and there are some iso- lated specimens from the fourteenth century; but its most productive period on the Continent was the sixteenth century (page 10).

This style of work came to England through the ecclesiastical route. It is known that the nuns of Little Gidding were expert at this type of embroidery early on, but it is not known whether they introduced it, although they are sometimes given credit for doing so. These nuns were best known for their beautiful book bindings.

It may be possible to trace English embroidery further back than that of any other national group. A chasuble that dates back to around A.D. 800 is the oldest known Western embroidery. Aelflaed, the wife of Edward the Elder, owned a stole and maniple made as early as 900. And, of course, no embroidery in the world is better known or more admired than the magnificent pieces of the *Opus Anglicanum* period in the thirteenth and fourteenth centuries. Most of these embroideries were executed in silks and metals and their technique shows the greatest skill and refinement. Some of this work shows intervals that are filled not only with the formalized scrolls, eight-pointed stars, and quatrefoils that were so well liked in that period, but also with magnificently worked beasts, flowers, insects, and birds.

In fact, it is interesting to note that English embroideries of all periods have included animals scattered about, flowers in isolated sprigs, caterpillars, butterflies, and various nameless insects to fill in the open spaces of compositions. Stumpwork, which enjoyed a very limited period of popularity from 1600 to 1700, was no exception. This curious endeavor, which can best be described as a combination

 (continued on page 24)

This picture shows very clearly the myriad stitches used in stump-work. The four flower motifs in the corners are "slips" worked in various stitches on fine mesh and then appliquéd onto the back-ground. Courtesy, Museum of Fine Arts, Boston. The Elizabeth Day McCormick Collection.

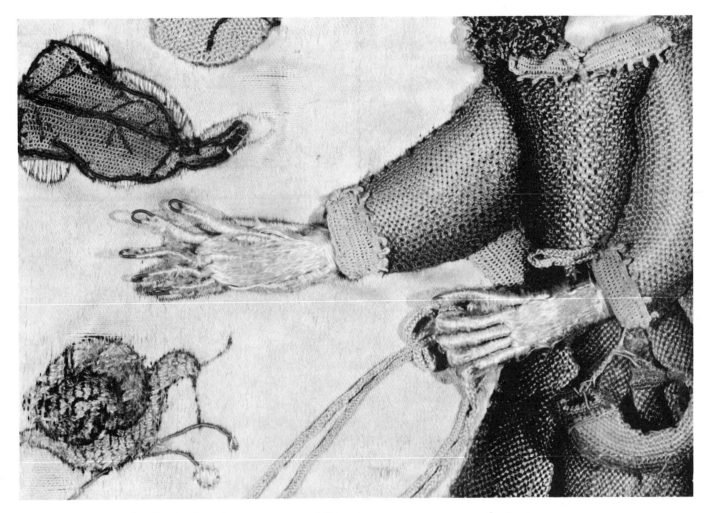

A detail of the photo opposite. This shows a common method of working. A wire frame is oversewn with silk to shape the hands. The gentleman's cloak is worked in burden stitch. This detail shows how carefully each part of the composition was attended to. Courtesy, Museum of Fine Arts, Boston. The Elizabeth Day McCormick Collection.

This could very well be a stumpwork sampler, a trial piece for a larger work. It has the stag and the tiger, well padded and raised; a solitary lady sitting on a beautifully worked mound, contemplating a huge rose; a "slip"; birds, trees, insects, and the ever-present cloud and sun—everything a meticulous embroideress would want to try out before attempting her masterpiece. Photo by Hallam Ashley. Courtesy, Strangers' Hall, Norwich, England.

Four designs which are very typical of the seventeenth-century "slips."

17

This small picture, entitled "Flora," is worked almost entirely in split stitch with silk and purl on a silk background. The rockery is done in very fine trellis stitch and the lion's mane in equally fine split stitch. The figures are only slightly raised. The degree of raising or padding seems to be at the worker's whim. Some examples are padded so highly as to be grotesque, with all sense of balance and proportion lost, while others are nearly flat. Many of these Stuart pictures, boxes, mirror frames, and book bindings are entirely flat. Many of them are worked in tent stitch on fine canvas. Although the designs are the same as those of stumpwork, here the resemblance ends. Courtesy, Museum of Fine Arts, Boston. The Elizabeth Day McCormick Collection.

OPPOSITE:
This typical piece is dated 1686. Note especially the small pony or horse in the right foreground. The roof of the King's tent is a fine diaper pattern, as is a section of the castle. There is a good bit of canvas work in this example. Victoria & Albert Museum.

Here are four "slips" worked, ready to be cut out and placed on the satin ground. The plum and pear present no problems in doing this; the cherry example is only a little more difficult; but the holly piece with all its angles and small units is a real test of skill. See pages 22 and 23. Courtesy, Museum of Fine Arts, Boston.

21

49.1898

Plate 1

Plate 3

Plate 2

Plate 4

Plate 1. *This is a most beautiful casket with many unusual details, a few of which are shown here. The man in* Plate 2 *has a movable wrist!* Plate 3 *shows a table set for feasting; platters of food are neatly arranged on a freestanding tablecloth.* Plate 4 *contains much material and a great deal of stitchery.* Courtesy of the Metropolitan Museum of Art, Gift of Irwin Untermeyer, 1964.

Plate 5. *The front of a casket worked in familiar units. An unusual feature is the introduction of a family shield, probably that of the workers.* Courtesy of the Metropolitan Museum of Art, Rogers Fund, 1929.

Plate 6. *This is an interesting example of stumpwork because it is unfinished and shows how the background was stamped on the fabric. This mirror surround tells the story of Sarah and Isaac. Among the motifs that fill the spaces are a nut tree with a squirrel, pomegranates, an iris, pears, a monkey eating a piece of fruit, a parrot on a tree sprig, and a beautiful kingfisher.* Courtesy of the Victoria & Albert Museum.

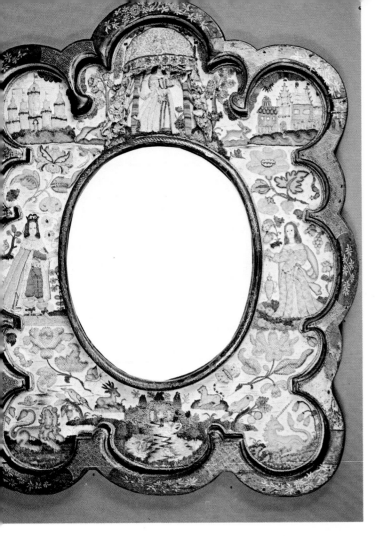

Plate 7. *This mirror surround is very typical. The oval glass is set in the center of the embroidered surround, which is framed in imitation Chinese lacquer. At top center is a figure under a canopy; on the left is an elaborate castle, and on the right is a less elaborate one. At the sides are the figures of a King and Queen. In the vacant spaces are the usual animals and plants and a fishpond. These looking glasses were valued highly. In 1649 Charles I had "a large looking glass sett in a frame of needlework."* Courtesy of the Victoria & Albert Museum.

Plate 8. *This is an unfinished design for a shaped frame. The top shows a house with flowers, trees, and the familiar sun. At the bottom is a very elaborate fishpond—this one even has a fountain. Spring, Summer, Autumn, and Winter are pictured in the four corners. Diana and Paris are also to be found on this piece.* Courtesy of the Victoria & Albert Museum.

Plate 9. *This mirror surround, which hangs in the John Paul Jones house in Portsmouth, New York, was made by Frances Wentworth. Frances, the daughter of Samuel and Elizabeth Deering, was born in Boston on September 30, 1745. She was married in 1769 to Governor John Wentworth of New Hampshire. After they moved to England, she became a lady-in-waiting to Queen Charlotte. On the back of the mirror is a paper that reads, "This embroidery was done by Frances Wentworth previous to 1776." The central figure is generally accepted to be Queen Charlotte.*

Plate 10. *A modern piece by the author, which employs all the old techniques. Silk, metals, and pearls are used. The King's canopy is in very fine tent stitch appliquéd to the background and edged with gold cord.*

Plate 11. *A garden scene, unusual in that the figures show little padding, while the fruit is worked over wooden molds and many of the tree leaves are detached. The bird in the upper right-hand corner is very fine silk cord; the dog, chenille. The women's collars are picoted and partially detached, their dresses made from rich materials. The gentleman is beautifully dressed in the mode of the time.* Courtesy of Mary Atwood.

Plate 12. *A small mirror surround, with very elaborately worked figures. The castle is raised as well as the figures. Silks, metals, pearls, and artificial flowers are used in this piece.*

Plate 13. *Here is a stumpwork picture using American motifs, worked by the author for the Bicentennial. The figures are dressed in colonial costume and the background motifs were taken from an American sampler dated 1745.*

Plate 14. *Jane Zimmerman worked this small piece in beautiful, meticulous stitchery. The lady's scarf is intricately worked with metal threads and beads. See drawing on page 44.*

Plate 15. *This piece has some marvelous touches: the cherries are worked over wooden beads, the door to the castle opens, the windows are glass, and the butterfly's wing is freestanding as are the flags waving proudly from the castle's battlements. The lady's underskirt is carefully embroidered with tiny stitches and the lady's bouquet is made up of tiny beads. Worked by Claire Gingras.*

Plate 16. *A completely up-to-date piece of stumpwork designed by Barbara Eyre and worked by the author. (See drawing, page 75.) All the old techniques are employed in the working, but the design is definitely twentieth century.*

Plate 17

Plate 17 *and* Plate 18. *These pictures show how stumpwork techniques can be translated into other media. Audrey Francini made this scene in an enchanted forest, working mostly in wools.*

Plate 18

23

of painting, sculpture, and embroidery, shows an abhorrence of any open space whatsoever!

Where did the royalist embroideresses—because this work was done almost entirely by the aristocracy—get their designs or design ideas? The more examples of this work are studied, the more it seems likely that they came from kits similar to those of today. The kits quite possibly contained the heavy white satin background, already stamped, and the necessary materials, but doubtfully any instructions for working. For example, a piece of woven material, a fragment of which was found in a work box decorated with stumpwork, appears again on the lid of the box and also on the lid of another, similar box. On two different pieces of work the same kind of material appears in the King's robes. And similarities of design and material appear at every turn. Nevison says, "Great similarity between some of the pieces of raised work . . . may imply that the designs were sold ready sketched out." The method of stamping shows in the unfinished pieces. It appears to have been done much as we do it now.

An alternative to the kit concept is that these pieces were designed for the wealthy worker by a traveling designer who had patterns and all the necessary working materials with him. It seems probable that the beautifully carved wooden faces and hands used in many of the pieces were either furnished to the worker with the "kit" or could easily be purchased. It does not seem likely that so many individuals could have been fine wood carvers!

Margaret Swain says in her *Historical Needlework*: "So frequently do the motifs recur on these pictures, mirror frames and caskets (boxes) that it is thought that the designs could be bought ready drawn on to the satin though no proof is yet available. Certainly many of the cabinets (boxes) are made up to a stock pattern, even the secret drawers are in the same place. It would appear that once the needle-woman had completed the top, sides and drawer fronts, the work was returned to the shop from which the designs were bought, to be made up to a stock pattern, often lined with pink silk. This theory is strengthened by a letter found in the casket of Hannah Smith, now in the Whitworth Art Gallery, Manchester. Because of this letter, the casket may be regarded as . . . a key piece for these embroidered cabinets. . . . The casket, in colored silks, gilt and silver thread and

This is a splendid example of a box or casket. The hands and fingers are worked over wire as in the photo on page 15. Note how the dresses are arranged in careful folds and stand away from the bodies of the figures. Los Angeles County Museum of Art, Gift of Mrs. Gordon Knight Smith.

spangles on white satin, has comparatively little raised work: only a single figure on the lid which shows Joseph being raised from the pit and sold to the Midianite merchants by his brothers. . . . The familiar lion and leopard on either side of the top lock scroll are also in raised work. The front door panels are worked in fine tent and rococo stitch with seed pearls and show Deborah and Barak and Jael and Sisera. On the sides below the handles are Autumn and Winter, a man with a cat before a fire. Its value as a key piece rests upon the enchanting letter written by Hannah Smith:

> The year of Our Lord being 1657.
> if ever I had any thoughts about the time; when I went to Oxford: as it may be I may: when I have forgotton the time, to fortifi myself: I may look at this paper and find it: I went to Oxford; in the year of 1654 as my being there near two years. for I went in 1654; and stayed there in 1655, and I came away in 1656, and I was almost 12 years of age, when I went I made an end of my cabbinet, at Oxford and my——? and my cabbinet was made up, in the year of 1656 at London; I have written this to fortifi myself, and those that shall inquire about it.
>
> HANNAH SMITH"

The caskets or cabinets usually have four bulbous feet of metal or painted wood. In the front two small doors open to disclose a nest of drawers. Many have a secret drawer behind. Above is a deep lid, containing a box or a mirror. More often than not, on the floor of the inside well is a colored engraving. These boxes had various uses, such as for work boxes, makeup boxes, and writing boxes.

Design sources, whether the pieces were stamped by professionals or by the workers themselves, were in all probability the pattern books of the time. These pattern books began to appear in the sixteenth century on the Continent. One of the earliest was published in Germany in 1525 by P. Quental. It showed figures, insects, flowers, and animals. A book published in France by Jacques LeLoyne not long afterward became a great favorite with English workers. Peter Stent, who lived in London during the reign of Charles II, published several popular books of designs. He had for sale "Books for the Drafts of Men, Birds, Beasts, Flowers, Fruits, Flyes and Fishes," including one

The Hannah Smith box or "cabbinet" described opposite. The
Whitworth Art Gallery, University of Manchester, England.

book of birds sitting on sprigs—a very common motif in stumpwork —a book of beasts, and a book of flowers. Among his pictures were the four seasons of the year and the five senses—again popular stumpwork motifs. He also published designs for the King, Queen, children, and so on. Circumstantial evidence suggests that Peter Stent's books were very much in demand.

Richard Shorleyker published his justly popular *Scholehouse for the Needle* also about this time. It was advertised in this fashion: "Here followeth certaine patterns of Cut-workes; newly invented and never published before. Also sundry sorts of spots in Flowers, Birds and Fishe etc. and will fitly serve to be wrought, some with gould, some with silks, some with crewell in coullers: or other wise at your pleasure."

John Taylor, a poet of the time, wrote "The Prayse of the Needle," in which he said:

> *Flowers, Plants and Fishes, Beasts, Birds Flys and Bees.*
> *Hils, Dales, Plaines, Pastures, Skies, Seas, Rivers, Trees;*
> *Theres nothing neere at hand or furthest sought*
> *But with the Needle may be shaped and Wrought.*

He also published a book of needlework patterns. Taylor, it was reported, was not bashful about borrowing patterns from various sources, and his book, being very complete, was also very popular!

The choice of subjects was interesting—one wonders sometimes about the reasons for the choices. Many patterns were influenced by the tapestries that were so popular in Stuart England. Biblical subjects, like those in the tapestries, might include Adam and Eve, David and Bathsheba, Isaac and Rebecca, the finding of Moses in the bulrushes, or Esther and Ahasuerus. Other subjects include pastoral idylls, figures representing the seasons, the senses, poetry, music, and the virtues. Many of the most favored designs were connected with the Stuarts.

During the wars between Charles I and Parliament, the royalist ladies were fond of embroidering miniatures of the King (stumpwork figures as well as real miniatures) and working Charles's real hair into them. Mention is made in old papers of the granting of the monarch's hair for this purpose. *(continued on page 37)*

This beadwork basket, 23 x 18½ x 6 inches, worked in the last half of the seventeenth century, depicts Susannah and the Elders. This illustrates clearly the carry-over of stumpwork designs into other media. Susannah and the Elders are very clear copies as is the not-so-ferocious lion. Some of the beaded fruits and flowers are padded and raised. Somehow the effect is rather untidy, more so than in the stumpwork examples. Victoria & Albert Museum.

A panel of needlepoint lace depicting the Judgment of Solomon. Note how similar this design is to the designs used in stumpwork. Victoria & Albert Museum.

OPPOSITE:
This lovely piece is initialed M V and dated 1656. It pictures, as do many, David and Bathsheba—carefully dressed in the court dress of the period! The two figures under the arch are not raised at all, while others, such as the lady at the left center and the figures in the tents at the lower corners, are raised quite high. The fountain is especially beautiful with the figure at the top. Note the raised petals of the rose and the great variety of insects in the background. Victoria & Albert Museum.

30

Casket or cabinet, embroidered with scenes from the story of Joseph and His Brothers. The style of this casket is the classic one, the doors at the front opening to disclose a series of small drawers. The figures are not highly raised. The Metropolitan Museum of Art, Anonymous Gift, 1939.

This is an example of the padded technique popular in England in the late eighteenth century. The padded woolen cloth bears no resemblance to the delicate technique of stumpwork. Victoria & Albert Museum.

This picture of Esther and Ahasuerus shows the King under an elaborate tent. Note the small lions, done on canvas in colored silks and then appliquéd. A great number of stitches are used in this picture, among them fine tent, long and short, satin, split, stem, Gobelin, plaited braid, and rococo stitches. The Metropolitan Museum of Art, Gift of Irwin Untermyer, 1964.

This is supposed to be a representation of the marriage of Charles II. It has an especially fine border, filled with animals and insects. There are many interesting details in this piece: the male attendant's beautifully detailed cloak; the King's robe, necklace, and crown; the Queen's collar, and the carpet on which the King stands. The fabric at the back of the King's throne is often seen; it must have been very commonly used. The Metropolitan Museum of Art, Gift of Mrs. H. H. Shearson, 1937.

This mirror frame or surround, on white satin, has three figures, two castles, two large animals, and many small animals, birds, and insects. The lady with the lute is found in other stumpwork pieces; it was apparently a popular motif. The pond in the lower center is especially good, as is the working of the two castles. The Metropolitan Museum of Art, Gift of Irwin Untermyer, 1964.

Much symbolism is supposed to be apparent in these pieces, and allegories abound. Animals—the stag, the tiger, the lion, and the unicorn—were well liked. Birds, insects, both real and imaginary, and caterpillars fill a multitude of vacant spaces on the satin ground. Some people have read significance into these, believing them to be symbols of different things. Castles are prominent, tents with canopies and with curtains that draw, fishponds replete with fish, the sun, the moon, and the clouds—almost any motif could appear in a piece of stumpwork.

Then again, crowded settings were the taste of the period and the embroideries perhaps followed the fashion. However, the caterpillar and the butterfly, so often seen, were known devices of Charles I. The oak tree was supposed to symbolize the hiding of Charles II in an oak tree. And various other motifs used extensively can somehow be related to the royal house.

The embroidery technique on these quaint pieces is above criticism. It seems as though nothing was beyond the capabilities of the gentlewomen of the time. They had, as has been noted before, the finest of materials, and the quality of their needles had improved. Silk was imported directly from the Middle East and metals from the European continent. Many household accounts of this time list the purchase of embroidery supplies. Besides ordering supplies such as these, one of the most famous of all needleworkers, Mary, Queen of Scots, also asked for "an imbroiderer to draw forthe such worke" as she would be occupied about.

Because in stumpwork parts of the design were thrown into high relief—the little figures, the animals, the fruits, birds, and various other motifs of the whole—while the rest was worked flat on a satin ground, a very uneven surface was produced. This made stumpwork useful for only a small number of objects—work boxes or makeup boxes (called caskets or cabinets), mirror frames (surrounds), book covers, and pictures.

Untold study, loving care, and expertise were lavished on these pieces by those who, as has been indicated, had leisure to spare. Great ingenuity was exercised and infinite pains were taken on the smallest details. The worker's delight in the bright, gay world in which she lived was mirrored in her work. All female personages in the embroideries, no matter whom they were supposed to represent, were always attired in the very elaborate dresses worn by the embroideress herself. The embroideries were excellent illustrations of the fashions of the times. Many an allegorical or biblical figure was dressed as would befit a king or courtier of the 1600s!

In a book published in 1894, *Old English Embroidery* by Frances and Hugh Marshall, the following description of working stumpwork is given: "The relief given to the figures was obtained by padding the raised portions with cotton wool or hair . . . thus throwing out the figures a good height above the grounding. The figures and ornaments were worked on linen tightly stretched on a small frame: when completed they were backed with paper to prevent the edges fraying and sewn onto the ground. Sometimes the figures consisted of several thicknesses of linen, the ground being worked with silk and the figures appliqué, thus gaining greater richness of effect by the added thickness. A great variety of effects was obtained by the different arrangement of the stitches used for the gold threads in the diapers of the backgrounds and other decorative details. The gold thread used was made by twisting a thin ribbon of gold and silver gilt around a silk thread."

A few details of this description need clarification. The linen was not unlike our linen twill. The figures were padded, each section individually, with hair, cotton, or wool held in place with crossed stitches. This foundation was covered with beautiful lace stitches or with bits of brocade, lace, or other adornments. Another way of producing the raised effect, used more frequently on animals than on human figures, was to work the animal in split or long and short stitch, again on a strong fabric. After working, the animal was cut out, leaving at least 1/4 inch all around. This was turned under and seamed to a like piece that was not embroidered. A small hole was left open and through this the cotton or whatever was pushed. When the figure was raised sufficiently, it was sewed up and then stitched to the ground.

These methods are in use today with one small exception: paper is no longer pasted to the back for cutting purposes. Today colorless nail polish is painted around the entire figure for about 1/4 inch, and when the polish is dry, the figure is carefully cut out.

 (continued on page 68)

A mirror surround. Again we find the striped material, here in the King's attire. Some thought was given to the composition of this piece; note that the mound at the top is exactly the width of the mirror frame. As is usual, no space has been left unfilled. The variety of fillers used never ceases to amaze. The Minneapolis Institute of Arts, Washburn Fund.

Top of a stumpwork box embroidered with figures in the style of the Stuart kings. In the background are a Stuart castle, a leopard, a lion, a beautiful dove, trees with many detached leaves, a branch of strawberries, and a full sun amid clouds. The figures are especially well dressed, mostly with materials. The same materials seen on the King's and attendant's clothing are seen on the King and Queen in the photo on page 35. The faces are worked on a wooden mold over which fine white silk is glued and then painted. Hands are also carved, but not covered, merely painted. The handle of the Queen's umbrella is a wooden stick wound with floss; note the detached tassels on it. The Queen has a necklace of real pearls. The Metropolitan Museum of Art, Gift of Mrs. Thomas J. Watson, 1939.

*Box opened to show the padded interior with perfume bottles and
a mirror.* The Metropolitan Museum of Art, Gift of Mrs. Thomas
J. Watson, 1939.

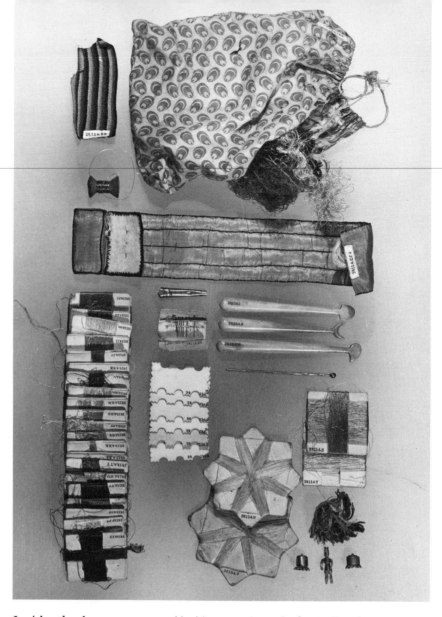

Inside the box on pages 40–41 were found the following objects: twenty-one paper winders marked *A P*, four unmarked winders, a bodkin marked *A P*, three ivory embroidery tools, a carved ivory doll, a spool of gilt thread, a silk tassel, a painted paper leaf, several skeins of silk, a metal cap, a metal puncher, a silk needle case, a piece of crinkle silk, a cloth bag containing scraps of silk, and a fragment of striped material that is found with amazing frequency in the stumpwork pieces. This piece is blue, but it is also seen in gold and pink or rose. It is thought that the *A P* might be the initials of Lady Ann Paulet, who was known for beautiful embroideries. The Metropolitan Museum of Art, Gift of Mrs. Thomas J. Watson, 1939.

OPPOSITE:

This picture representing the Judgment of Paris is a theme that recurs fairly often in stumpwork. The raised parts show very clearly in the photograph. The figures are beautifully dressed in elegant materials, needlepoint lace stitches, much knitting, and French knots. The Metropolitan Museum of Art, Rogers Fund, 1911.

Here is a nice pair suitable for pictures. There is much scope for imaginative stitchery in these designs. The man is leading the dogs and the woman is in the garden with the unicorn. These were adapted from the drawing on page 73.

Background into which the man opposite will fit.

Background for the lady on page 44.

Stumpwork box or casket, initialed S V, with a miniature garden in the lid. On the left door Abraham kneels before an angel; behind him is Sarah at the door of the house, which has mica windows. The faces and hands are of carved wood. On the left side Eleazer gives betrothal gifts to Rebekah. The drawer fronts have geometric flowers in laid work. The miniature formal garden includes ivory figures. Victoria & Albert Museum.

47

Possibly only the figures would be raised in this design, although parts of the fountain could be also.

OPPOSITE:
This is dated 1660 and shows King Ahasuerus and Queen Esther. The King is sitting under a canopy as the Queen advances toward him. Both are holding scepters. The King's attendant holds his staff. A woman attendant holds an umbrella over the Queen's head (see photo on page 40) while another carries her train. The faces of the figures are padded satin with embroidered features. The hands are delicately worked in split stitch. Both royal crowns are flat metal thread outlined with pearls. The Queen's umbrella is silk needlepoint lace outlined with metallic thread. The leaves, butterfly, veil, and various parts of the clothing are split stitch very finely worked. The castle, of couched silk and metal threads, has windows of mica. Some of the flowers and insects are in silk petit point. The lion is done in fine silk cord, couched. The tiger is in French knots. Real pearls, beads, and bits of glass are used to embellish an already ornate scene. The Metropolitan Museum of Art, Gift of Mrs. H. H. Shearson, 1937.

This is a beautiful example of the seventeenth-century picture. The cavalier and his lady are dressed faithfully in the costumes of the times. The flower basket at the center bottom is an unusual motif and offers the worker many choices in its execution.

This picture represents Solomon and the Queen of Sheba. Note how beautifully the Queen is dressed in lace. The central five figures are all raised, with carved wooden faces and hands covered with silk. The medallion frame and the castle above it are worked in purl, the rest of the picture in silks. The windows of the castle are mica, the eyes of the animals glass beads, and there are beads embedded in the rocks. Note the disproportionate size of the hands. Again, an umbrella is being held over the Queen by an attendant. The Metropolitan Museum of Art, Bequest of Carolyn L. Griggs, 1950.

OPPOSITE:
This picture, worked by May E. Periz in 1681, is a typical example. The central unit is quite elaborate. Note that the kings in the lower corners are under the familiar striped material. The sun is handled in an interesting manner. Minneapolis Institute of Arts, John van Derlip Fund, 1947.

This beautiful example, which is of much better design than most, having been taken from a Martin De Vos print, depicts the Return of Jephthah, who is greeted by his daughter. This is an unusual piece because it is worked on petit point instead of the traditional white satin background. Several examples have been found of raised work being done on petit point rather than satin. This picture is full of interesting details. Jephthah's daughter and her maids are playing lutes. The Elders of Gilead in the background have on Roman costumes and are depicted before their tents. The foreground figures are raised, the rest worked very finely in a great variety of stitches. The saddle of the horse at the right is applied velvet. The Metropolitan Museum of Art, Bequest of Irwin Untermyer, 1974.

OPPOSITE:

This looks as if the embroideress worked many "slips" for stumpwork pieces and then, finding them pleasing to her eyes, arranged them on a ground of satin and metal threads. The motifs are worked in silk on canvas in the traditional manner. The Metropolitan Museum of Art, Rogers Fund, 1913.

Compare this beadwork basket with the example on page 29. These bead-work baskets, nearly all in traditional stumpwork designs, while not espe-cially beautiful, are certainly tributes to the worker's skill. In this example the figures are especially well done. The Metropolitan Museum of Art, Gift of Mrs. Thomas J. Watson, 1939.

OPPOSITE:

The stumpwork surround of this mirror tells the story of Jael and Sisera. It is signed and dated A P 1672 on the back of the mirror. The center top shows Charity and her three children under a canopy of striped and shaded pink silk which has been applied to the back-ground fabric. In the lower center is a charming mermaid admiring herself in a mirror. The four corner medallions, a griffin, a cock, a camel, and a stag, are excellent. On both sides of the mirror are oval medallions, Jael on the right, Sisera on the left. Both are elaborately dressed in court costume. "Slips" fill the spaces between medallions. The side medallions are bordered with paper ribbon wound with floss and plaited. Among the attached parts are the mermaid's tail, the butterfly's wings, and the petals of some of the flowers. The striped material of the tent canopy is seen in blue and gold as well as the pink shown here. The mirror and its surround are framed in tortoiseshell. The Metropolitan Museum of Art, Gift of Mrs. Thomas J. Watson, 1939.

The figure and the leopard in this design are raised; the cherries and the rabbit can also be raised if desired. Detached flower petals and butterfly wing are at worker's choice.

In this design the figures would be raised, the bird unit if desired, and possibly the saucy deer. The two flower units could be handled as "slips."

The purse for the Great Seal of England, embroidered in silk and metal thread on silk. The raised parts are quite high, and the animals' bodies are fine silk cord, couched down. Beautifully worked. The Metropolitan Museum of Art, Gift of Mrs. Kalman Haas, 1923.

Details. The two male figures, both representing kings, have robes trimmed with like material. One of the kings stands under the familiar striped tent. This striped material apparently was very common. The Metropolitan Museum of Art, Gift of Mrs. Thomas J. Watson, 1939, and Gift of Irwin Untermyer, 1964.

This charming little box or casket originally stood on four ball feet. The figures on the lid are quite highly raised, those on the front doors less so. The camel on the right door is unusual. The back of the box features applied "slips" of exotic flowers and insects. The inside is lined with pink silk and velvet (nearly all of these boxes are). There is a sunken well lined with mirrors which has a hand-painted print pasted on the bottom. The three small drawers over one long drawer are also covered with pink velvet, while the doors are lined with pink silk. Colonial Williamsburg, Williamsburg, Virginia.

OPPOSITE:
This small picture—it is only 12½ x 18 inches—is elaborately framed. The animals seem especially spirited even though they follow common patterns. Two central figures are very carefully dressed and the center "slip" beautifully worked in rococo stitch. The Minneapolis Institute of Arts, Gift of Mrs. C. C. Bovey, 1929.

*This mirror surround is smaller than most, being only 19½ x 16½
inches with mirror size 9 x 12 inches. It also has a very unusual
shape. It is worked mostly in split stitch with metal bullion and silk
cords to embellish. Unusual parts of the design are raised, such as
the berries, the heads representing the sun, moon, and wind, the
fountain, and the chairs of the King and Queen. The royal personages are beautifully delineated entirely in split stitch, with some
metallic threads as well. Courtesy, Mary Atwood.*

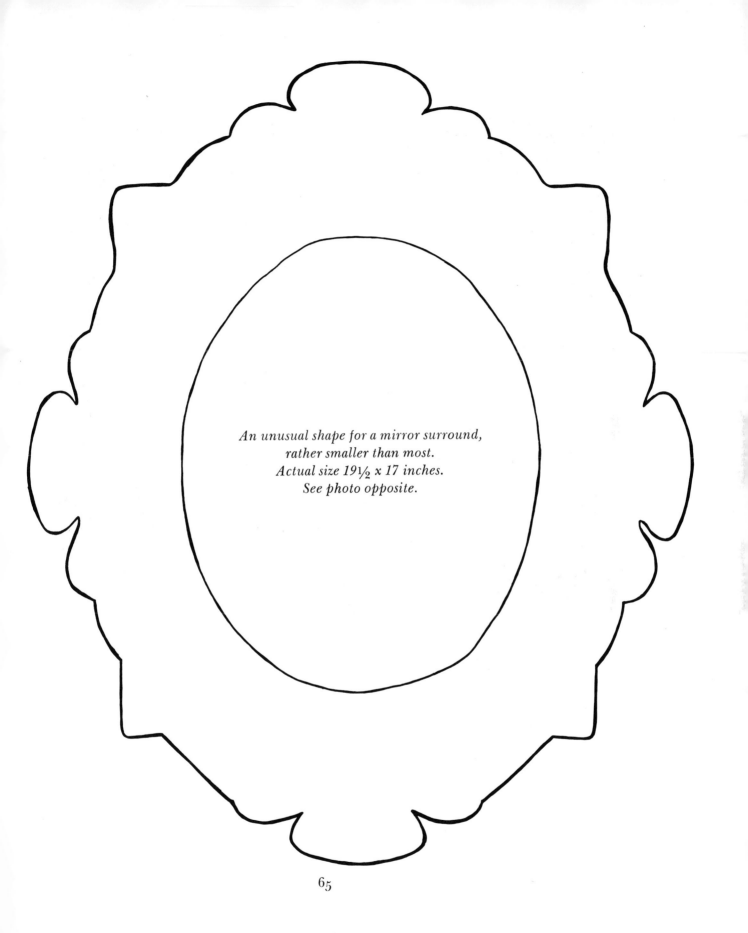

*An unusual shape for a mirror surround,
rather smaller than most.
Actual size 19½ x 17 inches.
See photo opposite.*

*This picture shows little raising and what there is, is not significant.
It is typical of the period, however, and has many of the usual units.
The castle, worked in silks, twisted floss, and metallic threads, has
mica windows. It is worthy of note that even in Stuart times stumpwork pieces were very much esteemed and were looked upon as
rarities. When Charles I wanted to make a special gift, he often chose
a piece of stumpwork.*

OPPOSITE:

*This stumpwork picture, worked by Rebeckah Wheeler in "ye month of
May 1664" and so labeled on the back, is said to be the earliest dated piece
of American needlework. Rebeckah was nineteen years old when she worked
this picture of the story of Esther and Ahasuerus. It is quite probable that
she got her design from England, as it is very like other known examples of
the same story.* Concord Antiquarian Society, Concord, Massachusetts.

Stumpwork: The Art of Raised Embroidery

So-called slips were worked in tent or rococo stitch on very fine silk mesh canvas or counted thread material, cut out, using the paper method to keep them from fraying (nail polish is used today), and carefully placed in the deplored open spaces. These were often elaborate flower sprays such as the ones illustrated on pages 21 and 22.

Another favorite "slip" was a bird in a cherry tree. The cherries in these were made over tiny wooden molds. Often they were simple wooden beads, but sometimes they were more carefully delineated—perfect little wooden pears, apples, and cherries are seen. The stitching over these molds is flawless and often shows a great deal of shading. Detached buttonhole was a favorite stitch, worked very finely.

The wings of birds and butterflies and the petals of flowers were often semidetached, or free-standing, as it were. To make a butterfly wing or a flower petal, work stitchery on flat surface first. Then work your choice of stitchery on the front and back of a wing-shaped piece of material or fine mesh canvas. Long and short and reversible stitches are especially good. Put front and back pieces together, working buttonhole stitch over a piece of fine wire that has been inserted between the two pieces. Attach in place. The mechanics may be covered with stitchery.

Most of the little figures are worked about half-round, but some are more nearly three-quarters and some are almost flat. It is not unusual to meet with all three varieties in the same piece. Possibly this was an attempt at perspective—an attempt that failed miserably, as there is no perspective at all in these pieces! Faces and hands were handled in various ways other than being carved. Sometimes they seem to be soft sculpture, but the finest were worked in split stitch over a small amount of padding. Many varieties of handling the faces are often found in the same piece, almost as if the worker were deciding which method she liked the best.

OPPOSITE:

This box's dimensions are W 15½ x H 9½ x D 12½ inches. Originally used as a toilet case, it is banded with tortoiseshell and has gilt ball feet. On the lid are four women representing the Four Seasons. These are highly padded and beautifully clothed. Each holds an appropriate attribute. The panels, including the two doors, are decorated with figures of a cavalier and a lady, angels and saints, a fountain, flower sprigs, animals, and buildings. A colorful print lines the bottom of the well. Inside the top compartment was found a long, narrow, parchment-bound book with overlapping flap and brass clasp. It contains accounts of monies expended on behalf of one Mr. Whitton of Tedington, with earliest entries dated 1682. This casket is said to have been given by Charles II to Mr. Whitton, Ranger of Wood-stock. Colonial Williamsburg, Williamsburg, Virginia.

A canvas-work purse of the seventeenth century, showing how the raised technique of stumpwork could be used in other forms. The purse is worked in silk and silver threads, seed pearls, metal loops and coils, mostly in detached buttonhole. The colors used include deep blue, pale blue, emerald, pale green, and pink. The grapes are of all colors and in high relief, and they completely cover the pink background. Victoria & Albert Museum.

Stumpwork

John L. Nevison, on page 23 of his *Catalogue of English Domestic Embroidery*, says that some of the colors used in stumpwork have interesting names. These names were taken from a sample list of the colors available:

Carnacon	*Drake*	*Isabella*
Watchet	*Tawnye*	*Beasar*
Murrey	*Clodie*	*Brassell*
Dove		

In the same list were such familiar names as

Gold	*Black*	*Crymson*	*Redde*
Silver	*White*	*Orange*	*Blew*

to name just a few. Nevison says, "On the whole, the most popular colors for embroidery would appear to have been dark and pale blue, shades of green, cream, pale yellow, pink, crimson, and black for the silk."

The split stitch was one of the favorite stitches and it was worked to perfection. Some other favorite stitches include:

French knot	*Basket filling*
Bullion knot	*Buttonhole filling*
Chain	*Buttonhole filling—knotted*
Outline	*Open buttonhole filling*
Buttonhole	*Buttonhole filling—spaced*
Cross	*Detached buttonhole*
Feather	*Wheel buttonhole*
Satin	*Raised chain band*
Trellis	*Cloud filling*
Ceylon	*Detached chain*
Hollie Point	*Fly*
Couching	*Long and short*
Bokhara couching	*Wave*
Turkey knot	*Raised buttonhole*
Burden	*Pekinese*
Needleweaving	*Plaited braid*
Braid	*Raised stem*
Step	*Raised fishbone*
Roumanian couching	

It was a period of self-expression and it would be hard to disprove the use of any of the threads, stitches, and so on, that people of the seventeenth century had—which is most of what we have now. As there were no books on "how to do stumpwork," ideas depended on the imagination of the worker and her neighbors.

A typical stumpwork picture such as the one shown here would show a man and woman, padded and raised, with hair styles and clothing typical of the period. The clothing might be evolved from beautifully executed stitchery or it could be made from bits and pieces of elegant materials, carefully stitched. The little "dolls" could have real hair (some are said to have hair from King Charles himself) and they were often embellished with real gold and real jewels. In the background would be a castle or castles, complete with towers, battlements, and gaily flying banners. There would be a cloud with the sun coming through. There would be one or more raised animals, in this case a very coy stag and a pair of coach dogs. This small picture—it measures only 9½ x 12½ inches—boasts six slips, two of really overwhelming size! These slips were worked in tent or rococo stitch on very fine mesh, "slipped" onto the background, and carefully fastened down. This is an interesting combination of techniques, but typical of stumpwork, where almost anything goes! At the feet of the couple is a fishpond, this one with two fish swimming about. The fishpond reflects the taste of the times when most gardens had pools well stocked with fish. And in accordance with the abhorrence of vacant space, there are four flying birds, five flying insects, four caterpillars, and two snails. The two small trees, one by the castle and one sheltering the deer, are of couched-down coils of purl, a metallic thread, packed in very tightly. A similar effect can be obtained with small bullion knots. Every nook and cranny of the design is filled and, as in all stumpwork, proportion and perspective are unknown.

Studied properly, embroidery can be a guide to the period in which it was worked. It also provides pictures of the social history of the time. Certainly this is true to a large extent of stumpwork; it provides insight into the life, manners, dress, and customs of its brief period of popularity, the seventeenth century.

Some contemporary examples are shown on the following pages.

A very typical design which is described in detail above.

This is a "working" piece. The leopard and the lion have been worked and are ready to be backed and stuffed. The two figures have been padded and are ready for dressing. The method of padding is explained on page 103. The faces of the figures were worked in the following manner. A piece of cardboard (file card weight) was cut to shape and padded; then a stocking was stretched around it, brought to the back, where it was secured, cut off as closely as possible, and then secured in the proper place by stitching through from the back without piercing the stocking face, as this would cause it to run. Features are carefully added and the hair is worked partly over the face edges so that the face does not stick out.

OPPOSITE:
Stumpwork "updated," a fine modern design by Barbara Eyre. This piece, called "The Lady or the Tiger," after the famous short story by Frank R. Stockton, gives many opportunities for adapting the old techniques. See Plate 16.

This is an unusual doll, dressed up by Betty Barker for her stump-work piece. She is wearing Mrs. Barker's great-grandmother's wedding handkerchief. The handkerchief was disintegrating, and Mrs. Barker skillfully shaped the usable portions to make a charming dress embellished with pearls. The doll has real hair couched on with metallic thread. The doll is truly in the seventeenth-century tradition.

OPPOSITE:
This is another modern design by Barbara Eyre. The center flower is perfect for a "slip."

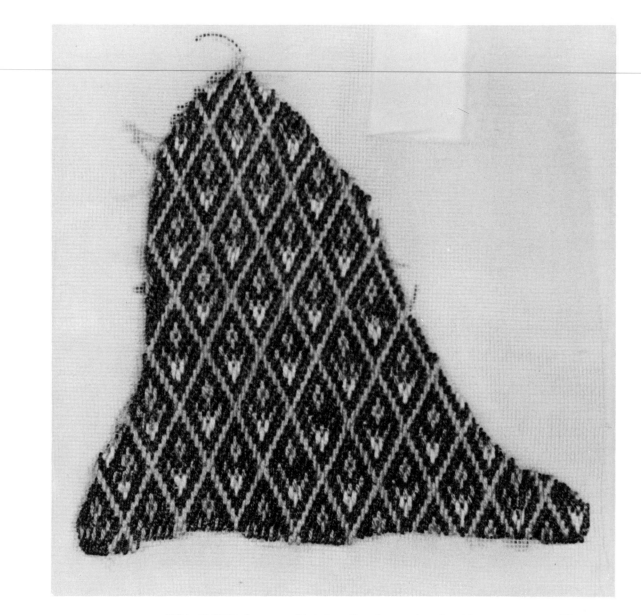

This "slip"—here a skirt for the figure in the photo on page 75—has been worked in pattern on fine silk mesh in silk thread.

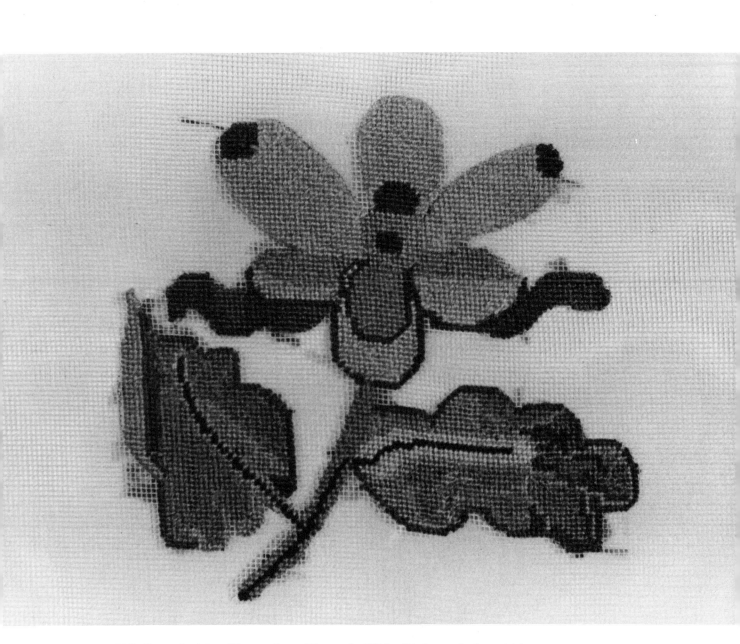

"Slip" worked in silks on fine silk mesh. This slip is ready for apply-
ing to the background. Colorless nail polish is painted about ¼
inch deep around the flower and leaves and allowed to dry thor-
oughly. Then, with small, sharp scissors, the slip is cut carefully
and closely, without snipping the threads. The piece is then ap-
pliquéd to the ground with blind stitches.

79

The raised petal on a rose, illustrated in large scale. To raise a petal, a butterfly's wing, or other small piece, first work the flat surface to which the raised part is to be attached. The raised piece will have two parts—front and back—which are worked separately. Each should be as much like the flat surface as possible. Insert a very small wire between the two parts and overcast the edges. Leave enough wire protruding at the bottom to weave to back and fasten.

A leopard properly stuffed and cut out. After the back is sewn up it is ready to be attached. First trace figure onto a piece of twill— two pieces, front and back. Work front as desired. Place front and back together and overcast, turning in raw edges. Stuff as shown.

The Stitches

BASKET FILLING

Alternate groups of satin stitches, spaced quite close together, horizontally and vertically.

BRAID

This stitch is worked from right to left. Make a loop. Hold the loop down, and insert the needle through it and into the material at the top. Then bring the needle out on the lower line immediately beneath after pulling the loop tightly. When this has been done, complete the stitch by drawing the needle through over the working thread. Continue to the next stitch.

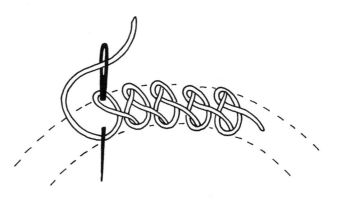

BRAID—PLAITED

This stitch is sometimes found in the garments of stumpwork figures. It is quite difficult to describe but fairly easy to work if the chart is followed carefully. It must be worked with a fairly stiff thread.

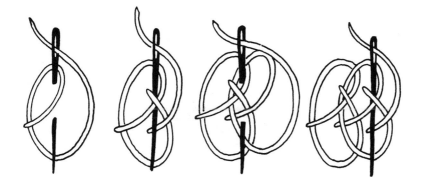

BULLION KNOTS

To begin, take a backstitch the size of the desired knot. Do not pull the needle through. Wind the thread around the needle as many times as necessary to fill the backstitch—five, six, seven, or more times; do not wind too tightly. Then, holding the coils with your thumb, carefully pull the needle through. Pull the threads until the stitch forms a neat coil. Insert the needle at X.

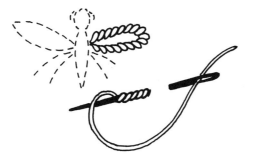

BURDEN

This stitch may be worked either closely or far apart. If far apart, it produces a beautiful, lacy effect. Lay parallel lines about ¼ inch apart. Then work a series of vertical lines between the first and third parallel lines, covering line 2. In the next row the stitches come up between the first row of vertical stitches, fitting in like bricks. Continue in this fashion until the shape is filled. Burden stitch is often used in tree trunks.

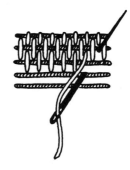

BUTTONHOLE

Bring the needle out on the edge that is to be raised and insert it at the opposite edge. Take a straight downward stitch with the thread under the needle. The next stitch should be taken as close as possible to the first.

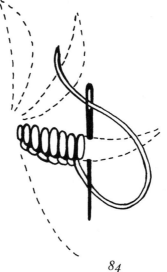

BUTTONHOLE FILLING

This stitch is used extensively in stumpwork. Work a row of back-stitches around the shape to be filled. Beginning at the left, work a buttonhole stitch into the backstitch. The next stitch is also a button-hole stitch, but upside down. Continue in this fashion until the right edge is reached. Reverse the stitches on the next row. Continue until the shape has been filled. On the last row work through the line of backstitches, thus securing the detached filling.

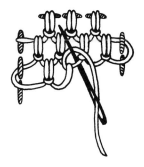

BUTTONHOLE FILLING—KNOTTED

Work a row of backstitches around the shape. Starting at the left, work a buttonhole stitch into the backstitches. A second buttonhole stitch is then made over the first, but at an angle. Pull the knot tightly. The second row is worked from right to left and the buttonhole stitches are reversed.

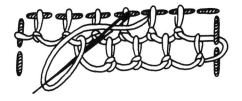

BUTTONHOLE FILLING—OPEN

First work a row of loose loops from left to right. All subsequent rows are worked into the loops formed by the previous row. Only at the edges of the shape does the needle enter the material. This stitch is a most useful one.

BUTTONHOLE FILLING—SPACED

Work rows of buttonhole stitches in groups of two, three, or four with spaces between each group. The needle enters the material only at the edges of each row.

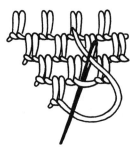

BUTTONHOLE—DETACHED

Work two stitches across the space to be filled. Starting at the left edge, work buttonhole stitches, placed close together, over both stitches. Work the next row from right to left. When the bottom is reached, stitches should be secured to the material. This stitch should be worked with a firm thread.

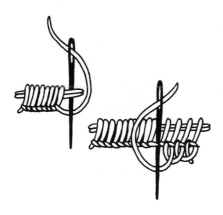

BUTTONHOLE—WHEEL

Work as any buttonhole, but each stitch goes into a middle hole. This procedure tends to enlarge the center hole, as can be seen in the diagram.

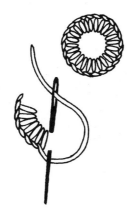

BUTTONHOLE—RAISED

Work a series of parallel bars about 1/4 inch apart. Work from top to bottom. Make a loop with the thread, then slide the needle under each bar without going through the material. This will make a buttonhole stitch. Proceed in this manner until the bottom of the ladder has been reached. Anchor the final stitch through the material.

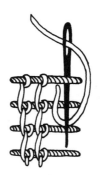

CEYLON

This stitch was often used in stumpwork. It gives the appearance of fine knitting. To begin, make a stitch from left to right across the shape to be filled. Return the thread to the left and come up just below the starting place. The thread is then looped into the straight line. The second row is worked from left to right.

CHAIN

Bring the thread out at the top of the line to be worked, and hold it. Insert the needle at the same point. Keep the working thread under the needle to form a loop. Pull both needle and thread through the loop.

CHAIN—DETACHED

This stitch is commonly known as the lazy-daisy. Bring the thread out where the stitch is to be made and hold it. Insert the needle at the same point. Keep the working thread under the needle to form a long loop. Pull both needle and thread through this loop. Tie down with a small stitch.

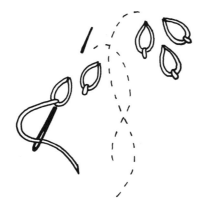

CLOUD FILLING

Make a series of small stitches at regular intervals (see diagram). Lace a thread into this foundation, first under an upper stitch and then under a lower one. The spacing may be varied.

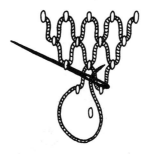

COUCHING

This is the simplest form of couching. It involves laying the required number of threads against the surface material and tying them down with small upright stitches, spaced at even intervals.

COUCHING—BOKHARA

In this form of couching the same thread is used both for the laid thread and for the tying-down stitches. Bring the thread out at the left and carry it across the shape to be filled to the right edge. On the return journey, from right to left, tie down this thread with a series of small slanting stitches.

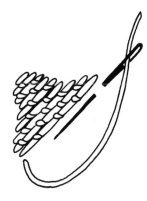

COUCHING—ROUMANIAN

This is worked exactly the same as Bokhara except that the tied-down stitches are long and slanting and almost indistinguishable from the laid stitch.

CROSS

This simple stitch must be done carefully. Make a small diagonal stitch. Cross it with another diagonal stitch. The top crosses must always lie in the same direction.

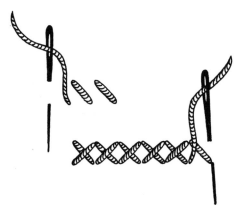

FEATHER

Bring the needle out at the center top of the space to be filled. Hold the thread down. Insert the needle a bit below and to the right. Take a forward stitch on a diagonal to the center, thread under the needle. Keeping the thread under the needle, place it to the left on the same level as the end of the last stitch and take a diagonal stitch to the center.

FLY

Bring the needle through *A* and down at *B*. Come up at *C* a little below *A* and *B*, and tie the thread down with a small stitch. Continue in this manner. This stitch may be worked from top to bottom or from left to right.

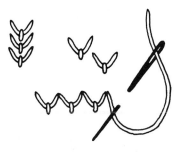

FRENCH KNOTS

Bring the thread out at the spot where the knot is desired. Keep the needle close to this place. Hold the thread down and wrap it around the needle, usually only *once*. Still holding the thread, twist the needle in the direction of the arrow and insert it at *X*. Release the held thread at the last possible instant.

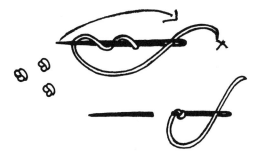

HOLLIE POINT

This was a very popular stitch with stumpwork embroideresses. It is actually a needle-lace stitch. The shape to be worked is outlined with chain stitch. Starting in the left corner, bring the needle out in the middle of a chain stitch. Hold the thumb over the working thread, which is wound around it from right to left. Insert the needle under the loop of the first chain of the top row. Then pass it under the first thread and under the loop on the left thumb as well. When the thread is pulled through, a small knot results. This sounds complicated but it works up easily.

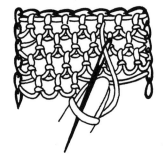

LONG AND SHORT

This is the most useful stitch for shading. Begin with a row of long and short stitches, the short stitch half as long as the long one. The next row of stitches bites up into the preceding row about one-third of the way up. These stitches are all the same length, but because the first row is uneven, this row will be also. Continue in this fashion until the shape is filled.

NEEDLEWEAVING

Lay two parallel stitches of equal size; the size depends on the shape to be filled. Come up at the top and start to weave on the two stitches. Do not go through the material. Go from right to left on the left thread and from left to right on the right thread. Pack these woven threads in quite tightly.

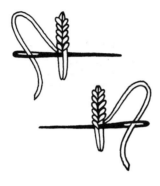

OUTLINE

Bring the needle out at the lower end of the line to be worked. Keep the thread to the left of (above) the needle and take a small stitch along the line to be covered. If the thread is to the right of (below) the needle, this is called stem stitch. Stem stitch produces a slightly thicker line than outline stitch.

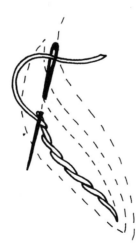

PEKINESE

This stitch has the effect of a small braid. Work rows of backstitches. Into these backstitches weave a thread, as shown in the diagram. Pull the resulting loops quite tautly.

RAISED CHAIN BAND

Work a series of foundation stitches fairly close together. This stitch is always worked from top to bottom. Bring the needle out just above the first stitch, pass it over the stitch and under it from below so that it comes out again at the top. Then take a blanket stitch on the right of the central stitch. Continue in this fashion.

RAISED FISHBONE

This stitch is used mostly on leaf shapes. Bring the thread through at the top of the leaf. Go through to the back on the center vein (see diagram). Come up at the left edge of the leaf opposite the point in the center where it entered. Put the needle down on the right edge near the top and bring it to the front on the left side exactly opposite. Now insert the needle a bit lower down on the leaf on the right side, then pass it horizontally under the leaf and bring it up on the opposite side. Insert the needle on the right side close to the second stitch and bring it up exactly opposite on the left side. Continue in this manner.

RAISED STEM

Lay a foundation of padding stitches vertically over the shape to be filled. Then lay a series of horizontal stitches at fairly close intervals. Then work stem stitch into these, beginning at the bottom.

SATIN

This is a difficult stitch to work well. Its beauty lies in flat, even stitches lying closely side by side. If possible, edge the shape to be worked in split stitch; this helps to keep the edge even. Carry the thread across the shape and return underneath the fabric to the starting point. It is best to begin at the center of the shape and work first to the right and then to the left. Satin stitch may also be padded. Lay layers of satin stitch in opposite directions—the last layer should lie in the opposite direction to the finished surface.

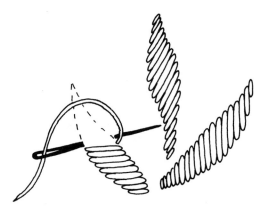

SPLIT

On the line to be worked take a small forward stitch. On the next stitch split the first stitch about a third of the way up. This makes a neat, flat line that looks not unlike a tiny chain stitch.

STEP

This is a fairly complicated stitch. The first step is to work vertical rows of chain stitch at either edge of the shape to be filled. Work horizontal stitches at an equal distance apart into these chains. Begin at the upper left. Wrap the horizontal threads five or six times. When the center is reached, carry the stitch a little higher up and then pass it through to the back of the material about $\frac{1}{8}$ inch above the bar. Bring the thread through to the surface in the correct position for continuing the wrapping stitches. The second row is worked as the first except that when the center is reached, the thread is passed around the long single stitch. The needle enters the material only at the start and finish of these rows.

TRELLIS

Work a row of chain stitches around the shape to be filled. Start at the top left-hand corner in the center of a chain stitch. Move to the next chain stitch to the right and slip the needle under this stitch. Do not pull the thread quite tight. This will form a small loop. The needle is slipped under this loop from left to right and then the thread is pulled tight, forming a knot. The needle enters the background only at the edges; the other stitches are completely detached.

TURKEY KNOTS

Put the needle down at *A*. Bring it up at *B*. Leave about 1 inch on top. Keep the thread below the needle and put the needle down at *C*. Come up in the same hole as *A* and pull tightly, holding onto the loose end. In the next step keep the thread above the needle and go down at *D*. Come up at *C*, but do not draw the thread tightly, thus leaving a loop. Now, with the thread below the needle, go in at *E* and up at *D*. This time pull tightly. Repeat. When finished, cut the loops to form a soft, velvety pile.

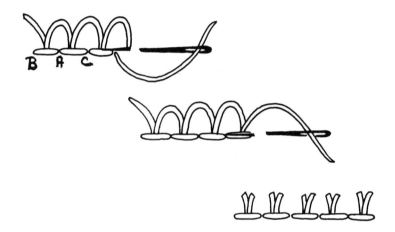

WAVE

Work a row of satin stitches across the shape to be filled, quite close together. Begin at the right side. Weave the working thread under the base of satin stitch. Do not enter the material. On the downward movement pick up a small stitch and then slip under the next satin stitch, which is just above. Continue in this manner. It is possible to make this stitch very open simply by spacing the first row of satin stitches more widely. It makes a lacy filling.

Another modern design of great appeal—"The Little Drummer Boy"
—designed by Judith Savage Becker.

The lady and the unicorn, worked by the author.

How to Do It, Step by Step

1. Place the figures of the lady and the unicorn on linen twill or another strong fabric. Stretch tautly in a frame for working.

2. Pad the figure of the lady, except for hair, face, and hands, with polyester filling or cotton batting. Pad each marked section separately. Tie the stuffing down with crossed stitches ✕ ✕ . Sections may be padded to different heights for textural effects.

3. Work hands and neck in flesh-colored silk using split stitch and three strands of thread. (Mouline may be used instead of silk.)

4. The face is also worked in split stitch. If you desire, cut a piece of file-card-weight cardboard to shape, pad it, and stretch a piece of stocking over the padding. Draw the stocking to the back, secure it, cut off excess material, and attach the face to the figure from the back. Make sure that no stitches penetrate the stocking face, as this could cause it to run. Features are put on in silk—very carefully, as they cannot be picked out. French knots are used for the eyes and straight stitches for the eyebrows and mouth.

5. The hair could be real hair, couched down with invisible or perhaps metallic thread. It should be styled in the fashionable seventeenth-century manner. Or the hair could be fashioned from either bullion knots or French knots. If you use the cardboard method of making the face, be sure that some of the stitches go over the edges to ensure a melding of the face and hair.

6. The lady is now ready to be dressed, in stitchery or in bits of lace and rich materials. Either or a combination of both would be in keeping with the best seventeenth-century tradition. After dressing, she may be embellished with beads, feathers, and gold. Old bits of costume jewelry can be broken up and used; these add a great deal to the composition.

7. Paint colorless nail polish all around the edge of the figure, extending it about ¼ inch. Paint both sides of the material and be sure to reach all parts of the figure. Allow it to dry thoroughly. Take a pair of small, sharp scissors, and *carefully* cut out the figure, watching that you do not cut the threads or materials. The raw edges will show; paint them with a dark brown or black felt-tip marker. Put aside.

8. Work the unicorn in split stitch. (The one in the picture is made of satin and is less typical.) Back with the material on which it is stamped. Cut it out, leaving the back open for the necessary stuffing. Sew it up and lay it aside.

9. Work the background on heavy white satin or peau de soie. Antique satin also works well for more modern pieces. Use any stitches that please you and that enhance the design. Don't forget the possibilities of metallic threads and such variety threads as purl. (The mound under the unicorn is purl.) Birds' wings could be detached, as could the bravely flying banners. The bouquet of flowers could be small flowerettes sewn together. Small pieces of glass could be placed behind the castle windows. The three large leaves on the right could be worked flat and then worked on material or canvas and attached to add dimension. Study the plates for ideas.

10. After you have completed the background, sew the lady and the unicorn in their proper places.

11. All work *must* be done on frames, as it is impossible to block stumpwork.

See photograph page 112.

A Stumpwork Box

IN AN OLD BOOK published in London in the late 1800s (*Old English Embroidery* by F. and H. Marshall) is a detailed description of how a stumpwork box was worked. It is interesting and helpful in showing what stitches were put where.

". . . the faces and hands of the figures are carved in wood and worked over with long stitches, the King's curtains are real lace, and the various bows, loops and strings on the sleeves, shoes and at the necks and waists of the little ladies and gentlemen are all of real braid. But, with the exception of a few eccentricities of this kind, the work is good and delicate, and the designs most quaint. The use of purl in many of the flowers and in the houses at each end of the box, is varied and effective.

"The box is remarkable for having one or more figures on every panel, as they must have been troublesome to execute; and it is also very noteworthy that the name of the worker—Ann Greenhill, March the 21, 1677—is embroidered on the front of one of the drawers inside.

"It is fitted up as a workbox, and the divisions and drawers are all worked over with silk threads kept very long.

"The colours generally are much faded, but enough is left to show what they originally were. . . . The entire box, top and sides, is edged with a broad border of tortoiseshell, the rich colouring of which forms a most effective frame for the delicate handiwork within.

Front of Box.

"The greater part of the work is in buttonhole or lace stitch, generally applied over a thickly-padded groundwork, but sometimes used
alone, as in the petals of the rose on the lid, and in the tulip, carnation
and butterfly on the front.

"The front opens with two doors, adorned with a little lady and
gentleman. The lady wears a bodice of white satin embroidered with
a flower in blue and green, a pink skirt and sleeves, and blue petticoat.
Blue bows of narrow braid are at her neck, on the sleeves and shoes
and in her hair and she has a white openwork collar. On the same
panel are a white carnation, a white and yellow butterfly and a tree.
The cushion is blue with a yellow edge. The gentleman wears white
with pink braid bows on his shoes; a yellow and white tulip, a brown
stag, and a tree are on the same panel. The mat or carpet is black and
white. Along the top there is a blue bird, a brown rabbit and a green
parrot with red wings and various leaves and flowers.

Lid of Box.

"The lid has a design, apparently representing King Charles II and
his queen, Catherine of Braganza, with a page supporting her train.
The King stands under a canopy of striped yellow and white silk, sup-
ported by two pillars and having curtains and a cornice of green, pink
and yellow lace. The steps of the alcove are white, worked over with
yellow silk and flanked by two lions couchant. The back is hung with
a white curtain bearing a design, in colours, of fleur-de-lis. The king
wears his crown and a large wig, white lace bands and deep colour; his
red and white striped cloak is lined with feathers, probably representing ermine, and his dress is pale brown. The bows at his knee and in

the white shoes are green and white braid, and the cushion between his feet dark green. The queen is also crowned and wears an elaborate white satin dress, embroidered in feather stitch with flowers and leaves; she has loops and bows of pink braid at her neck and on her sleeves; her train is white, worked in open ovals with a yellow edge and the collar white lace. The royal emblems of the rose and the thistle are worked in their proper colours, except that the rose seems to have been white with a red edge; but this may be faded. The castle is in blue and grey silk, with a blue door.

"The back of the box has in the lower panel a fountain with two basins, the upper one pale yellow, the lower one coloured purl. The center column is yellow satin, covered with open white lace, the top white and blue in lace stitch. The lions' heads are yellow, and the water worked in wavy lines of blue and white silk. On the right of the fountain is a sportsman in grey, with a blue hawk on his wrist, at his neck and shoulder blue bows; on the left is a lady in a blue striped dress and white petticoat spotted with black; she has pale pink ribbons

Back of Box.

in her hair, at her neck, and on her sleeves. Next to her is a tree in French knots, with a little brown monkey at its base and on the opposite side another in coloured purl. On the top panel is a spirited design of a white greyhound chasing a brown rabbit, a butterfly and thistle at either end worked in many-coloured purl and in the centre a group of strawberries in purl and lace stitch.

"The side panel to the right has a lady dressed in white with pale green bows, holding a flower in her hand; she is accompanied by a brown dog with a yellow collar. The house is all worked in purl of different colours and the oak tree of natural colours in purl lace stitch and a thin metal thread for the stem; the large pink flower is worked in lace stitch and purl. The caterpillar is all coloured purl. At the top is a floral design in purl and a brown squirrel in the centre with a chenille tail.

"The side panel opposite shows a lady in a very elaborate dress of many colours, wearing a white petticoat, with yellow braid on the bodice, sleeves, waist and neck; she is an old lady which is uncommon in work of this kind. The house is of many-coloured purl and the oak tree is made with French knots. The top panel has in the centre a grey rabbit in lace stitch, at one end a snail and at the other a bee and between them sprays of flowers, all coloured purl.

"The box is 13½" x 11" x 7½"."

Side Panel.

Side Panel.

A truly lovely piece of modern stumpwork, worked by Elizabeth Richter in stitchery worthy of her predecessors. The unicorn is worked in split stitch, beautifully shaded, and the lady wears a velvet dress.

Bibliography

ALFORD, LADY MARIAN. *Needlework as Art*. London: Sampson, Low, Marston, Searle & Rivington, 1886.

BAKER, MURIEL. "Stumpwork," *Needle Arts*, vol. 1, no. 3, 1970.

BURTON, ELIZABETH. *The Pageant of Stuart England*. New York: Charles Scribner's Sons, 1962.

CHRISTIE, MRS. ARCHIBALD. *Samplers and Stitches*. London: B. T. Batsford, 1934.

CUNNINGTON, C. WILLET AND PHILLIS. *Handbook of English Costume in the 17th Century*. London: Faber & Faber, 1955.

HUGHES, THERLE. *English Domestic Needlework*. New York: Macmillan, 1961.

HUISH, MARCUS. *Samplers and Tapestry Embroideries*. London: Longmans, Green & Company, 1913.

JOURDAIN, M. *English Secular Embroidery*. New York: E. P. Dutton & Company, 1910.

KENDRICK, A. F. *English Needlework*. New York: Charles Scribner's Sons, 1933.

LOWES, EMILY. *Chats on Old Lace and Needlework*. New York: Frederick A. Stokes Company, 1908.

MARSHALL, FRANCES AND HUGH. *Old English Embroidery*. London: Horace Cox, 1894.

NEVISON, JOHN L. *Catalogue of English Domestic Embroidery*. London: Victoria and Albert Museum, 1938.

SELIGMAN, A. SAVILLE, AND HUGHES, TALBOT. *Domestic Needlework*. London: Country Life, 1926.

SWAIN, MARGARET. *Historical Needlework*. New York: Charles Scribner's Sons, 1970.

SYMONDS, MARY, AND FREECE, LOUISA. *Needlework Through the Ages*. London: Hodder & Stoughton, 1928.

THOMAS, MARY. *Mary Thomas's Dictionary of Embroidery Stitches*. London: Hodder & Stoughton, 1965.

TREVELYAN, G. M. *Illustrated English Social History*, vol. 2. London: McKay, 1942.

Judith Savage Becker stitched her lady's scarf to look like fur and made an elaborate headdress of pearls and metal threads.

Index